C000178929

Your *shagathon-based* workout

'You could put a blond wig on a hot-water heater and some dude would try to f**k it.'— *Tina Fey*

This edition published in 2020

By SJG Publishing, HP22 6NF, UK

© Susanna Geoghegan Gift Publishing

Author: Michael Powell

Cover and contents design: Virtual Gin Party

ISBN: 9781912295869

Printed in Croatia

10 9 8 7 6 5 4 3 2 1

Contents

Disclaimer

Every page of this book uses language and describes activities that would not only make your grandmother blush but also her bondage-loving lesbian mistress. *Some of them are in violation of the law if actually carried out.*

We do not advocate the breaking of any law. This information is for humorous purposes only and frankly, it's crazy that we should have to formally point this out to cover our arses.

We don't guarantee that any of the material contained in this book is correct, workable, factual or even funny.

We are not responsible for, nor do we assume any liability for, damages resulting from your monumental stupidity if you choose to follow any of the information contained here within. Except this disclaimer. We want you to follow that. But nothing else, from here on ... starting NOW!

Have you ever had sex? Isn't it great?

It's definitely one of the three best things you can do with your body (the other two are interpretative dance and becoming an organ donor – not necessarily in that order).

Sex is so awesome, it's no wonder that we think about it so much, that our popular culture is obsessed with it and that we spend crazy amounts of time and effort chasing it. We just can't stop trying to do all the sex.

The good news is, sex contains no artificial colours, flavours or preservatives and is mostly suitable for vegetarians, although it may contain nuts. It strengthens the immune system, improves libido, eases stress and boosts sleep (right guys!).

But did you know that sex can also help you to lose weight? It burns five times more calories than not having sex. Think about that the next time you're sitting in church, on the bus or just visiting your granny.

Shagging™ and eating – these two activities are vital for the continued existence of the human species and yet both are as much maligned and misunderstood as they are enjoyed.

So this revolutionary book has analysed 45 sexual positions or scenarios. It reveals their calorie-burning potential and offers this remarkable body of knowledge to help you to get the body you've always dreamed of while you literally Shag Yourself Slim.

INTRODUCTION

#1 Knee Trembler

When two people, usually drunk, try to have a quickie in a stairwell or down an alley, counting calories is the last thing on their minds. However, if you find yourself in this position, allow the smell of urine and desperation to bring you back into the present so you can make the very most of your brief encounter.

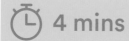 **4 mins**

Calories burned:
Knee tremblers are by necessity so short that the weight-loss benefits are practically non-existent. However, the aftermath may have dramatic consequences for your health such as catching an STI or discovering that the thieving little scrote you just boned has stolen your wallet.

Weight loss bonus:
+200 kcal (70g smoked pork bratwurst) brewer's droop or being moved on by the police.

-400 kcal (1.3kg low fat cottage cheese) hurl on the pavement.

-400 kcal (400g light chicken and cheese enchilada soup) walk home or sleeping on a bench in the park.

-350 kcal (1.6kg mushrooms) visit to the walk-in clinic.

Motivational thought:
The worst sex I've ever had has always been great.
Vince McMahon

Did you know?
In a recent study of 7,455 people from the USA, Dubai, China, France, Germany and India, 51 per cent said they could go longer without sex than they could go without coffee.

KNEE TREMBLER

#2 Break-Up Sex

The jury is out on whether or not break-up sex is a good idea. Detractors argue that it's emotionally confusing; supporters say this is exactly what makes it so hot, plus it can help couples to achieve closure. When one door slams shut another door opens, and it's usually the fridge, so anything is preferable than comfort eating an entire tub of Rocky Road, right?

 **6 mins**

Calories burned:
Break-up sex is tinged with mindfuckery and regret but it's usually a breathless quickie that skips the foreplay, so it burns a few calories efficiently, plus you don't have to cuddle afterwards.

Weight loss bonus:
+3,500 kcal (13 cups of ice cream) if you're only having sex to win your partner back. When they've gone you're going to hit the fridge harder than an NFL linebacker.

+5,000 kcal (24 brandy buttercream mince pies) if you split over Christmas – a fridge full of festive goodies is going to be your new bae.

Motivational thought:
Break-up sex is like a trifle that's been dropped on the carpet – it's better to leave with dignity than sit on the floor scooping jelly and custard into each other's faces.

BREAK-UP SEX

Did you know?
Physical attractiveness is
associated with a higher likelihood
of getting divorced and men who
cheat are likely to have lower IQs.

#3 Frotting

Frotting means to rub or chafe and refers to people rubbing their body parts together, but it has particularly come to be identified with the practice of rubbing/holding/fapping two dumbsticks together for sexual pleasure; it's a good option for guys who don't enjoy anal.

 20 mins

Calories burned:
Collectively it should burn the same calories each as solo pleasuring (about 25 kcals each) because it involves the same number of hands per dick, but if you put two people in a kayak, one of them usually ends up doing most of the work, so it's probably an 80:20 split.

Weight loss bonus:
-15 kcal (45g Brussels sprouts) if you cross the finish line together.
-20 kcal (55g cooked minced beef) for 'docking' (putting helmet inside partner's wizard's hat – use plenty of lube).
-20,000 kcal (31 jumbo hotdogs) for the sheer effort of staying in the closet afterwards.

Motivational thought:
It's not really masturbating if you're jacking your clone off. It's more like politics.
Jarod Kintz

FROTTING

Did you know?
Technically, two 'bros' flicking each other with wet towels and then slapping boners together ('sword fighting') after a rugby match also comes under the frotting umbrella, and there's nothing gay about that at all.

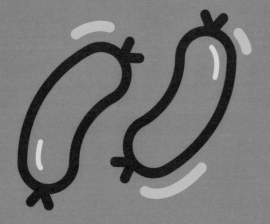

#4 Cottaging

Anonymous sex in a public lavatory can be a great way to lose weight, especially if it's one of your major hobbies, because that means you're doing it at least two or three times a week and have already established a healthy weight-loss routine. Hiding in the bushes or running from the police can also burn a few dozen calories.

 **10 mins**

Calories burned:
Sex in a confined space uses extra energy, but if the risk of getting caught keeps your encounters brief, then the weight loss benefits will be greatly reduced. In fact, you'd see better results if you spent all evening beating off in front of a computer screen.

Weight loss bonus:
-50 kcal (7 stalks of celery) if you have to evade arrest.

-1,500 kcal (15 mini cheese corn quesadillas) if you spend a night in the cell, miss breakfast and are then bailed pending trial.

-20,000 kcal (117 bowls of porridge) for early release after three months in prison.

Motivational thought:
I am always looking for meaningful one night stands.
Dudley Moore

COTTAGING

#5 Dogging

If you enjoy having sex in public in front of strangers, then you just have to flick through the rest of this book to find how many calories you will burn. However, if you're a spectator, then your weight loss opportunities depend solely on the contents of your thermos flask and picnic.

 **90 mins**

Calories burned:
Tramping through secluded woodland to watch strangers get it on in a car park can really work up an appetite – all the more reason to bring healthy snacks. So, it's no to the pork pies, cocktail sausages and scotch eggs and hello to sliced veggies with lashings of homemade Baba Ghanoush. Ah, that unforgettable after-dusk aroma of smoky grilled aubergines is so evocative of horny couples, belly bumping in their sporty hatchbacks.

Weight loss bonus:
-100 kcal for nutritional portable snack choices such as avocado toast, Brussels sprout chips, cucumber sushi, keto-friendly hot chocolate, etc.

-400 kcal (9 large wedges cantaloupe melon) if you skip breakfast the following morning to compensate for those late-night calories.

Motivational thought:
There are few things so pleasant as a picnic eaten behind the recycling centre on the A38 near Taunton, whilst the entertainment is laid on by the locals.

WARNING – Did you know?
Dogging currently remains <u>illegal</u> in
the UK. People caught dogging can
be <u>prosecuted</u> under the Sexual
Offences Act 2003 or for outraging
public decency.

DOGGING

#6 Butterfly Position

The woman lies on her back on the edge of a bed or table and either places her feet on the man's shoulders or around his waist, while he stands or kneels upright facing her. He tilts her hips upwards with his hands, or she could be propped up with a pillow underneath her lower back.

 6 mins

Calories burned:
The man does most of the work but the woman can control her level of activity. If it's her birthday, she can let him do everything (not too passive or he might as well be boning the table), or she can burn more calories and get more pleasure by controlling the height of her hips so that he hits her G-spot.

Weight loss bonus:
-85 kcal (4 jumbo shrimp) for him, just for showing up.

-65 kcal (5 medium shrimp) if she uses her abdominals to keep her legs raised.

-50 kcal (half a finger of Twix) for her if he finds her G-spot.

Motivational thought:
Butterfly is ideal for men with tiny dicks, as it allows greater penetration and stimulation of her inside lady parts.

Did you know?
Butterfly is a good position to use if you want to conceive; the pelvic tilts also make it a recommended way to induce labour.

BUTTERFLY POSITION

#7 Giving Head

Bobbing your face up and down on a purple schwanz burns a lot of calories and requires good core strength if you're on your knees; cunnilingus is less calorie hungry unless your technique involves waggling your head like a wet spaniel rather than relying on your tongue.

 20 mins

Calories burned:

Half an hour of vigorous oral sex can burn up to 80 calories, the equivalent of a slow jog on a running machine. Faced with such stiff competition, it's a miracle that the fitness industry manages to stay in business, although its detractors say that giving head is to enter a cruel time vortex where ten minutes with a mouthful of junk feels like a hundred years.

Weight loss bonus:

+7 kcal per teaspoon (30g of coconut water) if you swallow.

+20 kcal (5g of cheese) if the receiver hasn't showered.

Motivational thought:

Giving head is good for your health.
Getting head is good for the soul.

Chloe Thurlow

Did you know?
In ancient Rome men tended only to receive, since giving head was considered a debasing act. In fact, a Roman court could order an offender to go down on the wronged party as recompense for a crime. Quid pro quo, bro.

GIVING HEAD

#8 Spooning

It seems so innocent – two people lying on their sides, he's on the outside gently nuzzling his body into hers; no pressure just a lovely warm feeling of security as they drift off to sleep. . . absolutely useless for burning calories until. . . hello, what's this? A boner pressing urgently into her back.

 10 to 180 mins

Calories burned:

The suspense is unbearable. Will they or won't they? If yes, then check the other pages of this book for calorific details; if no then refer to Onanism on page 64, unless he lies awake all night with blue nargberries.

Weight loss bonus:

-400 kcal (30 pecans) if you both fall asleep looking unbearably cute and wake up feeling refreshed.

-35 kcal (2 walnuts) if he knocks one out with quiet efficiency.

+400 kcal (360g tuna) if she wakes up, because then he'll have to wait until she falls asleep again and the resulting sleep deprivation may make him eat more tomorrow.

Motivational thought:

Sex is as important as eating or drinking and we ought to allow the one appetite to be satisfied with as little restraint or false modesty as the other.

Marquis de Sade

Did you know?
The 'love hormone' oxytocin
is released when two people
spoon, along with dopamine
and serotonin.

SPOONING

#9 Pool Sex

Sex in any body of water from a Jacuzzi to the ocean looks super hot, but it's fraught with risks. The chlorine in a swimming pool can really mess up the delicate pH balance of a woman's velvet lounge. Also, water isn't a lubricant, so laying pipe under these conditions can cause micro tears in skin and condoms, which also increases the risk of contracting an STI.

 **6 mins**

Calories burned:
You'd better be really into each other because without lubrication you could be in trouble. The best solution is to keep it quick, which reduces the risk of injury, but that also lowers the weight loss potential. You're looking at burning about 60 kcal max, unless you do get an STI, which will help you drop a few pounds, so it's a mixed bag.

Weight loss bonus:
-100 kcal (20 roasted peanuts) if the hot pool guy chases you away.

-200 kcal (2 sweet potatoes) if the hot pool guy joins in.

-400 kcal (132 cherry tomatoes) for the self-esteem boosting revelation that movies lie.

-1,000 kcal (5 cups cream cheese) for STI.

Motivational thought:
Sex is more exciting on the screen and between the pages than between the sheets.
Andy Warhol

Did you know?
Water-based lube will wash
away underwater, so use
silicon-based instead.

POOL SEX

#10 Foot Job

Since most of us possess a full complement of functioning hands, the foot job would appear to be a solution looking for a problem. But just as there will always be people who enjoy watching snooker, there are many who favour the arduous task of pleasuring their partners using just their feet.

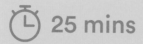 25 mins

Calories burned:
Foot fetishes aside, the self-imposed difficulty can be its own attraction, like bog snorkelling or deliberately ditching your starter Pokémon in Sword and Shield. Cranking one out pedally requires good core strength and burns about 100 kcals, twice as many as a straightforward hand job, as it takes a mighty effort to keep your feet together.

Weight loss bonus:
-50 kcal (1 large plum) if you keep your feet clamped to furnish a gratifying foot-vulva.

-5 kcal (125g asparagus) if you excavate their spadger with your big toe.

-5 kcal (30g cucumber) per minute of enthusiastic 'shrimping' (toe sucking).

Motivational thought:
Heaven is between our feet as well as over our heads.
Henry David Thoreau

Did you know?
Foot fetishism – podophilia – is the most common sexual fetish in the world, possibly because both the feet and the genitalia occupy the same cortical area in the brain.

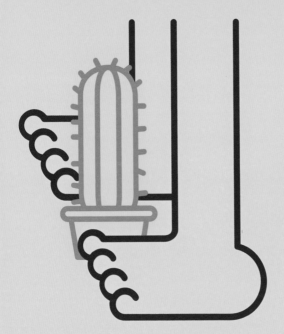

#11 Autofellatio

This is, of course, gobbling one's own bean or crank rather than enjoying the breakfast of champions in a car. Sadly, most people – nearly all women and 99 per cent of men – lack the monolithic body parts or circus background to perform this, but that shouldn't stop you burning a few calories in the attempt.

 8 mins

Calories burned:

This depends on your level of commitment. Award yourself 6 kcal for every minute you spend in convex frustration and +20,000 kcal for the three years of fruitless yoga classes. If only blind optimism alone could raise a person's metabolism, you'd be skinnier than Iggy Pop.

Weight loss bonus:

+7 kcal per teaspoon (7 leaves of romaine lettuce), if you swallow.

+450 kcal if you binge eat an entire box of Jaffa Cakes out of sheer exasperation.

Motivational thought:

Blessed is he who expects nothing,
for he shall never be disappointed.
Alexander Pope

Did you know?
According to ancient Egyptian
texts, the calorie-conscious god
Atum created the god Shu and
goddess Tefnut by fellating himself
and spitting out his own semen
onto the ground. You can bet they
got teased at school.

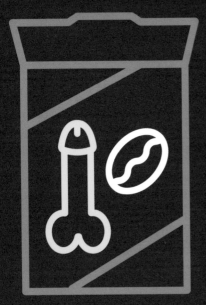

AUTOFELLATIO

#12 Dry Humping

Dry humping is the Versailles Treaty of sexual relations because it usually leaves at least one party feeling hard done by. Nobody dry humps because they want to; it's the gluten-free option, the least worst choice in the circumstances, either because someone's pretending to be abstinent, trying to overcome religious programming or simply doesn't want to go any further.

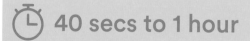 **40 secs to 1 hour**

Calories burned:
Visit any nightclub on a Friday night and you'll see fully-clothed strangers dismally grinding away on the dance floor, proving that dry humping gets more of an outing than it deserves because it's monumentally damaging to one's sanity as well as for losing weight.

Weight loss bonus:
-150 kcal (3 rich tea biscuits) if you manage to bring on the china.

-25 kcal (5 cherries) for the extra laundry.

+670 kcal (1 kg of blueberries) if sexual frustration sends you to the fridge to comfort eat.

Motivational thought:
There is always shame, pain, humiliation and frustration in waiting but in the end comes glory.
Endale Edith

Did you know?
Usually, getting lubed up is a plus, but during 'outercourse' friction is both your friend and your foe. Also, it's worth bearing in mind that a torn fraenulum can take two months to heal – that's the length of Columbus' voyage to America.

DRY HUMPING

#13 Erotic Accordion

The man lies on his back and brings his knees into his chest; the woman squats over him as if she's about to take a piss behind a dumpster, but instead she slowly lowers herself onto him. They lock eyes, try to block out the pain and pretend that their intertwined limbs and mutual discomfort constitute a mystic experience.

 4 mins

Calories burned:
He gets a core workout; she gets to control the vertical action but not her cramping thighs. If he could just pull up his damn knees a bit more, she might actually be able to find his peen. It's hard to judge the calorie burning potential of this deeply frustrating position because someone usually decides that it's too much effort.

Weight loss bonus:
-80 kcal (1 hard boiled egg) if you see it through to its disappointing conclusion.

-25 kcal (one third of a piece of part-skim string cheese) if she can resist blaming his tiny dick for the shallow penetration.

Motivational thought:
Welcome to Hell. Here's your accordion.
Gary Larson

EROTIC
ACCORDION

Did you know?
Accordions look fun but they're
fiendishly difficult to play, hence
the name, probably.

#14 Lotus Position

The man sits on the bed or floor with his legs stretched out in front of him and the woman straddles and faces him. It's basically cowgirl with the man sitting up rather than lying down. There's not much potential for thrusting for him, so she gets to control the action and have a more intensive workout.

 14 mins

Calories burned:
The woman burns most of the calories and gets a good core workout. She can grab the headboard and push sideways to tone her arms or throw them around his neck, kiss and caress or make fun of his bald patch (unless there's a big height differential, she'll get a good view of the top of his head).

Weight loss bonus:
-60 kcal (150g yellow onions) for the thigh, core and buttocks workout.

Motivational thought:
Be like a lotus. Let the beauty of your heart speak.
Be grateful to the mud, water, air and the light.
Amit Ray

Did you know?
Lotus is a sacred flower for Hindus and Buddhists and symbolises purity. Pink Lotus is the national flower of India. Individually wrapped Lotus Biscoff (38 kcal) are commonly found on hospitality trays at conferences.

LOTUS POSITION

#15 Teabagging

Teabagging is exactly the same as dunking a teabag up and down in a mug, except the teabag is someone's sweaty ball sac and the mug is your mouth. These homoerotic 'top bants' have bored fire fighters and post-match rugby players written all over them.

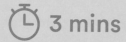 3 mins

Calories burned:

From a weight loss perspective it's a complete waste of time unless combined with squats – three sets of ten reps – for the teabagger, although it's hard to see how the teabaggee can derive any health benefits from this activity.

Weight loss bonus:

+10 kcal (30g watermelon) for salty balls.

-20 kcal (1 small date) for energetic ball sucking.

-75 kcal (10 almonds) if both guys wrestle for about ten minutes.

-25,000 kcal (500 small peaches) if the teabagger finally confronts his behaviour and decides to come out of the closet and stop living a lie.

Motivational thought:

... and then Gavin tea-bagged Josh at the back of the team coach it was awesome #ROFLCOPTR

Did you know?
You don't have to be into being
humiliated, or even identify as
kinky, to enjoy teabagging. It's all
about intention.
Sophie Saint Thomas

TEABAGGING

#16 The Spider

The man and woman sit, legs bent, leaning back on their hands and forearms. Then they shuffle into each other until their junk makes contact. They stare into each other's eyes as they bump and grind, secure in the knowledge that they're both equally responsible for making the fireworks happen.

 16 mins

Calories burned:
This is one of the most gender progressive positions in the erotic repertoire with both parties expending the same amount of energy relative to their body size, 80 kcal on average.

Weight loss bonus:
-25 kcal (11g turkey jerky) for face-to-face because appetite-suppressing oxytocin levels shoot up relative to the degree of intimacy.

-25 kcal (50 sunflower seeds) if you perform this position on a bed rather than the hard floor, because you'll have to work harder.

Motivational thought:
I believe in honesty. I believe in a good time.
I believe in good food. I believe in sex.
Bertrand Russell

Did you know?
The male dark fishing spider (Dolomedes tenebrosus) mates with just one female because ejaculation immediately kills him. She then eats him. Buzzkill.

#17 Foreplay

Ignore foreplay at your peril, but for health reasons, make sure it begins with some body-on-body action. Sex is a contact sport, so sharing a romantic meal doesn't count. If that's the only way you can get in the mood, you're doomed, because no amount of boffing will burn off a Nando's wing platter and large wedge of cheesecake.

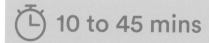 10 to 45 mins

Calories burned:
You can expect to burn about 25 calories for every 15 minutes of foreplay, so if you go for the full 45 minutes, that's one stick of part-skim string cheese or a 10-minute light jog. Sex only lasts for about 6 minutes, on average, so don't skip over the foreplay, which typically lasts for about 10 minutes (although women report they want twice as much).

Weight loss bonus:
0 kcal if you send her flowers or fill the dishwasher.

-1.6 kcal per minute of touching/kissing/licking/sucking.

-40 kcal (40g crab meat) if you deliver an erotic
full body massage.

Motivational thought:
Don't stint on foreplay – or afterplay. Be inventive.
Ruth Westheimer

Did you know?
For a male giraffe, foreplay consists of ducking his neck down to pat the female on her backside. This makes her urinate. He then drinks the urine (25 kcal) to see if she is up for it. After watching him drink her piss, she usually isn't.

FOREPLAY

#18 Body Sushi

Body sushi is the Japanese practice of serving sushi or sashimi on the nude body of a woman (Nyotaimori (女体盛り)) or less commonly, a man (Nantaimori (男体盛り)). It rose to prominence during Japan's Edo period (1603–1867) when plates went out of fashion and body sushi parties were common among the samurai class and organised crime rings like the Yakuza.

 15 to 45 mins

Calories burned:
Whether you view body sushi as an art form or a sexual fetish or both, you're certain to gain more calories than you burn, although it's one of the healthiest meals you can eat and those tuna rolls are irresistible!

Weight loss bonus:
-25 kcal (1 bell pepper) if you wear a gimp mask and remain nil-by-mouth.

-120 kcal (half a pint of bitter) if you accidentally rub wasabi sauce into your eyes or genitals.

-5,000 kcal (183 smoked salmon and cream cheese parcels) for any Streptococcal infection or STI.

Motivational thought:
Don't dunk your nigiri in the soy sauce. Don't mix your wasabi in the soy sauce. If the rice is good, compliment your sushi chef on the rice.
Anthony Bourdain

Did you know?
Sushi began as cheap fast food
and originated outside of Japan in
Southeast Asia.

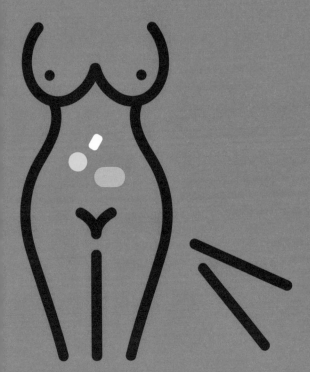

BODY SUSHI

#19 Hand Job

Whether you're a slum landlord with an insolvent tenant or your partner isn't in the mood for full coitus, the trusty palm dongler has a well-earned reputation for compromise and is a reliable way to literally and figuratively wipe the slate clean. The chub rubber inevitably gets a more active workout than the rubbee, especially if he or she delivers a fugue rather than a simple one-handed étude.

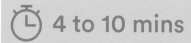 4 to 10 mins

Calories burned:

A perky handygram is a good forearm workout and burns about 50 kcals (one sixth of a McDonald's Original Cheeseburger) per sore wrist more per hour than passively having one's pork pulled.

Weight loss bonus:

-25 kcal (1 medium tomato) if the balls are in play or if the fraenulum enjoys a filigree of finger jibbling.

-40 kcal (1 cucumber) for a full prostate massage.

-50 kcal (1 oatcake) per hour for 'pepper grinder' or any other weapons-grade counterpoint technique.

Motivational thought:

A johnson in the hand is worth two in the shrubbery.

HAND JOB

#20 Mile High Club

The mile high club is a not-so-exclusive group of people who have had sexual intercourse on board an aircraft in flight. In a recent survey, 9 per cent of Americans claimed to have had a sexual encounter in an aeroplane seat, 17 per cent in the bathroom, 5 per cent with a stranger and 3 per cent with a crew member.

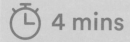 **4 mins**

Calories burned:
Sex in a confined space burns a few extra calories, but the risk of getting caught (it's actually illegal to have sex on a regular commercial flight) means that such encounters are generally super quickies, so you'll be lucky if you burn more than one nibble of a Twix finger. However, on the plus side, reduced oxygen levels in the cabin can lead to better orgasms.

Weight loss bonus:
-450 kcal (in-flight meal) if you miss the hostess trolley whilst humping in the toilet.
-10 kcal (3 breath mints) for contortions.

Motivational thought:
Good judgment comes from experience.
Unfortunately, the experience usually comes from bad judgment.

Did you know?
Pioneering aviator and founding
member of the mile high club,
Lawrence Burst Sperry, invented
the autopilot in 1914 so that
he could bone local socialites
under the pretext of teaching
them how to fly.

MILE HIGH CLUB

#21 Fisting

Anything grunthole related comes with a delicate care label.
Beginners: you should stretch your clay corridor gradually by
experimenting with a barrow load of vegetables accompanied
by gallons of veterinary-grade lube. That means arranging for an
experienced 'fisting top' to post fennel bulbs and raw beets into
your clacker for weeks before you even think about taking it up to
the elbow. You'll also need to learn how to breathe and relax.

 25 mins

Calories burned:
You'll probably want to increase your intake of fibre to maintain
regularity and to help promote digestive health, so that's a big plus
for your weight loss regime. Some aficionados of chuff-pipe glove
puppetry recommend psyllium fibre supplements when daily
fennel and beetroot salads eventually lose their lustre.

Weight loss bonus:
-1,000 kcal (415g of double chocolate gelato) if you're
allergic to latex.

-5,000 kcal (2,075g of double chocolate and raspberry gelato)
if your partner's other hobby is playing the guitar. You'll be
surviving on fruit smoothies for a month while the walls of your
Marmite highway heal.

Motivational thought:
Whoever is careless with the truth in small matters cannot be
trusted with important matters.
Albert Einstein

Did you know?
If you want to maintain an ultra-tight spadger, then fisting probably isn't for you, but you won't destroy your butt or end up incontinent, so long as you take it slowly, get lots of advice from skilled veterans and only play with people you trust.

FISTING

#22 Anal Sex

Although the LGBTQ community has been plying the mustard road for centuries, until recently cornhole drilling has been a guilty secret among heterosexuals. But now it's as commonplace for young, straight couples as holding hands under the table at a Harvester, albeit driven mostly by the porn-addled guys.

 10 to 25 mins

Calories burned:
The bottom burns 75 kcals (3 tablespoons of chutney); the top burns 100 kcals (a small chocolate brownie square). Anal is expressly not the same as doggie style with added bum fiddling. Be gentle, use plenty of lubricant and newbies, please stay in the shallow end.

Weight loss bonus:
-10 kcal (1 reduced-fat Pringle) per minute if it's painful.
-30 kcal (1 carrot) for the persistent worry of stress incontinence.
Drop a clothing size when you empty your bowels.

Motivational thought:
'The four most overrated things in life are champagne, lobster, anal sex and picnics.'

Christopher Hitchens

Did you know?
There's a high concentration of nerve endings around and just inside the anus so there's no need to go at it like you're burying a fence post. Think of gently mashing potatoes rather than operating a pneumatic tamping machine.

ANAL SEX

#23 Tantric Edging

'Edging', also known as 'orgasm control', is the practice of reaching the point of orgasm and then deliberately stopping before you spray the mayonnaise. It seems like the perfect way to develop facial tics and a stammer, but apparently it isn't harmful at all and increases the chances of achieving the elusive simultaneous orgasm.

 60 to 480 mins

Calories burned:

Prolonging your lovemaking is good because it uses more energy, but the more mystical you become about the whole business, the more likely you are to slow everything down. Eventually you'll be locked in a timeless embrace, as the universe sprinkles its blessings on your sacred immobile coupling, which is nice but it doesn't burn any calories. So stay real and use the gift of delayed gratification wisely.

Weight loss bonus:

+100 kcal (125g cottage cheese) for every activity you blow off whilst performing a marathon session (e.g. going to the supermarket, walking the dog, cleaning the oven, etc.).

-100 kcal (small latte with skimmed milk) for every hour that your lovemaking keeps you away from the fridge.

Motivational thought:

Electric flesh-arrows traversing the body. A rainbow of colour strikes the eyelids. A foam of music falls over the ears. It is the gong of the orgasm.

Anaïs Nin

Did you know?
Nobody likes a smart-arse, so if
you manage to achieve
eight-hour tantric sex sessions,
keep quiet about it.

TANTRIC EDGING

#24 Make-Up Sex

Make-up sex is super intense. You feel more connected than ever, you want to make it up to your partner for whatever it was that you did wrong and you hope it burns more calories than a recruitment weekend with the French Foreign Legion. But sadly, those conflicting emotions could actually scupper your weight loss goals.

 10 mins

Calories burned:
If you both keep active, then you can expect to burn 50 kcals each, but all that good work is likely to be destroyed by your new-found connection. This calls for a two-hour post-coital verbal dissection of your relationship and waffles for breakfast because you feel all cosy and loved up again. Finding your soul mate is bad for the waistline.

Weight loss bonus:
+100 kcal (3 medium figs) for earnest discussion, whilst lying prone and grotesquely inactive.

+175 kcal for each waffle with syrup.

Motivational thought:
You must learn to let go. Release the stress.
You were never in control anyway.
Steve Maraboli

Did you know?
Make-up sex is a good way for partners to reconnect, but if you rely on it regularly to interrupt or resolve arguments, then you're doing more harm than good. Studies show that stress hormones can actually interfere with your fat metabolism and make you gain weight, so it's better to resolve your conflicts verbally rather than between the sheets.

MAKE-UP SEX

#25 Bondage

From PVC straitjackets and handcuffs to spanking and pony harnesses, bondage offers so many calorie-burning opportunities that it's difficult to do the subject justice. Suffice it to say that the sheer practicality of consensual physical restraint is very appealing, since it's impossible to raid the fridge when you're suspended naked from the kitchen ceiling.

 30mins to 24hrs

Calories burned:
Many couples who use bondage as part of their healthy diet enjoy positive weight loss outcomes and it's not just those who are hog-tied for extended periods and can't fix a snack – gimp masks and ball gags also help to tackle those stubborn food cravings.

Weight loss bonus:
-300 to -800 kcals for each snack/meal you forgo whilst nailed to a bedpost.

If you explore equine play, by all means involve carrots, but avoid those calorific pony nuts, which although high in bran, contain rapeseed oil and molasses.

Motivational thought:
I don't remember reading about nipple clamps in the Bible. Perhaps you were taught from a modern translation.
E.L. James, Fifty Shades of Grey

BONDAGE

A 'munch' is a group of
people that enjoy kink
behaviour or lifestyle.
Ironically, the name derives
from 'burger munch' when
BDSM groups used to meet
up at burger joints during
the 1980s.

#26 Phone Sex

An advantage of sex 'à une distance' is that you can select your level of physical activity and your partner need never know. Whether you ride a cross trainer or exercise bike, eat a Lion Bar multipack, catch up on some housework or simply pummel yourself ragged with a giant dildo, the choice is yours.

 5 to 20mins

Calories burned:
10 to 35 kcals then add on whatever fat burning activity you're performing at the same time.

Weight loss bonus:
-10 kcals (3 grapes) if you manage to keep a phone wedged between shoulder and ear.

+1,076 kcals (Lion Bar multipack) for Lion Bar multipack.

-200 kcals (60g air-popped popcorn) for dildo nemesis.

Motivational thought:
If your conversations are becoming 80 per cent heavy breathing and 20 per cent talking, that's not a long distance relationship, that's a free phone sex hotline.

Did you know?
If you want to increase your chances
of having an orgasm, keep your
feet warm, according to research
at the University of Groningen in
the Netherlands, which increased
orgasms in a small test group from
50 to 80 per cent just by making
participants wear socks.

PHONE SEX

#27 Kebab Buster

After a night on the town, have a ride while you wait for your ride and burn off those stubborn takeaway calories with a quickie behind the bus shelter. Be careful not to drop your bag of chips.

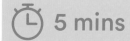 5 mins

Calories burned:
25 kcal summer (half a finger of KitKat)
46 kcal winter (1 McDonald's Chicken McNugget).

Weight loss bonus:
-600 kcal if you get arrested and spend a night in the cells and miss breakfast. Winning!

Motivational thought:
Shag smart for a healthy heart!

Did you know?
A teaspoon of pearlescent jizz contains more hipster gut bacteria than a gallon of Kombucha.

KEBAB BUSTER

#28 Pegging

Whether you use strap-on, strapless or a double-dildo kit, you're onto a winner when it comes to burning those extra calories. For maximum all-round benefits, choose a ribbed strapless, so that the receiver can enjoy quivery internal thrills with every thrust whilst the wearer gets a direct G-spot massage and improved kegel strength. Then you can reverse roles until everyone is fizzing out of their bungholes.

 50 mins to 4 hrs

Calories burned:
Since they aren't limited by the male requirement to recharge and reboot, two women can bump and grind all night, grab a couple of hours sleep, then have another steamy session before sharing a healthy breakfast of kiwi fruit and Greek style yoghurt. Or a bacon sandwich. They earned it. If you're a woman who's just given your male partner anal, he'll probably need breakfast in bed while his prostate recovers.

Weight loss bonus:
-100 kcal (4 slices of turkey breast) for the wearer.
-600 kcal (6 tablespoons peanut butter) if you pull an all-nighter.

Motivational thought:
I think the world will be a better place when more men take it up the arse. Once a guy has been on the receiving side of penetration, suddenly he really gets it.
Charlie Glickman

PEGGING

Did you know?
Pegging is also sometimes referred
to as 'Bend Over Boyfriend,' or
BOB for short, which originated
from the first educational video for
straight couples about male anal
penetration.

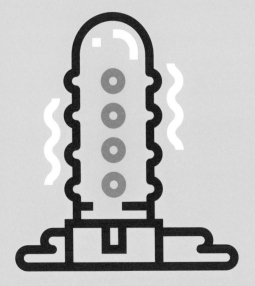

#29 Missionary Position

This dependable vanilla institution attracts much ridicule, but it burns some tidy calories, although the man-on-top can enjoy 3¼ times greater energy expenditure than the inert woman, who traditionally lies supine, silently fretting about a pile of ironing.

 25 mins

Calories burned:

105 kcal (6 large scallops) for the man.

32 kcal (4 almonds) for the woman.

Weight loss bonus:

-25 kcal (50 sunflower seeds) if she does the Viennese oyster (legs behind head).

-10 kcal (1 cashew) if she loudly and energetically fakes her orgasm.

+15 kcal (13g tuna) if she falls asleep before the vinegar strokes.

Motivational thought:

You are never too old and boring to have another orgasm.

MISSIONARY POSITION

Did you know?
During the Middle Ages, the missionary position was the only sexual position permitted by the church and Italian Dominican friar Thomas Aquinas declared all others a crime against nature.

#30 Onanism

Cracking one off relieves stress and aids sleep, but it only burns about ten calories. The only way it can significantly impact weight loss is as a substitute for snacking. Someone offers you a cup of tea and a biscuit? You graciously accept the hot beverage and then scuttle off to the bathroom to rub one out.

 3 to 45 mins

Calories burned:
Even though its many euphemisms imply vigorous activity, increasing blood flow to one's genitals need barely raise a sweat. But as a food replacement system it offers a free, easy solution to losing weight: have a healthy wank instead of breakfast, another for lunch and enjoy a regular meal in the evening.

Weight loss bonus:
-1,500 kcal (700g turkey jerky) per day: regularly tapping into your potential has the power to transform your weight loss dreams.

Motivational thought:
The good thing about masturbation is that you don't have to get dressed up for it.
Truman Capote

Did you know?
Onan was a minor Old Testament figure.
He wasn't caught celebrating Palm
Sunday; he was actually pilloried for
cumming on the tits of his dead brother's
wife because he didn't want to be
disinherited. But posterity records only
that he was a pre-eminent tosser.

ONANISM

#31 Swinging

If swinging was good for your waistline, then why is every documentary about this alternative scene crammed with obese middle-aged couples? The fridge is the fifth person in these people's relationships, so if you're interested in both swinging and getting trim, you need to ask yourself some tough questions about your lifestyle choices.

 90 mins

Calories burned:
Make sure you don't become the spare cog who has to settle for beating off whilst the other three have the time of their lives. Other than that, you'll probably lose a few more calories than you would with a stale old monogamous shag.

Weight loss bonus:
-50 kcal (5 cashews) because we all work harder to impress a stranger.

+650 kcal (5 scoops of whey) if you share a three cheese fondue or a platter of mushroom vol au vents (since you appear to be stuck in the 1970s).

Motivational thought:
In my sex fantasy, nobody ever loves me for my mind.
Nora Ephron

SWINGING

Did you know?
It's thought that in the United States of America, swinging began among American Air Force pilots and their wives during the 1950s before spreading to the wider population.

#32 Sixty-Nine

When two people go down on each other at the same time, they're of course said to be engaged in a sixty-nine, or as some prefer, the doubly euphemistic 'soixante-neuf'. Say anything in French and it sounds simultaneously sexier and less rude.

 **20 mins**

Calories burned:
Half an hour of vigorous oral sex can burn up to 80 calories, the equivalent of doing 400 jumping jacks or ten minutes of white water kayaking.

Weight loss bonus:
-50 kcal (2 small anchovy fillets) if you upscale to a 70 (one person stands wearing their partner like a gasmask, whilst he or she gobbles in an inverted position).
-25 kcal (half an Oreo) for the top.

Motivational thought:
A really good blow job is like making a cake, the gathering of ingredients, the mixing and stirring, the slow baking in the warm oven of your mouth. Timing is everything.
Chloe Thurlow

SIXTY-NINE

Did you know?
The Kama Sutra calls this position
the 'congress of a crow' even though
so far these highly intelligent and
adaptable birds have never been
observed giving each other blowies.

#33 Cucking

If you get pleasure from watching your neighbour bone your wife, then it will also thrill you to learn that they get all the aerobic benefit while you sit in the wardrobe trying to coax your cuckolded joystick into a lacklustre semi. After he or she has finished giving her a good consensual seeing to, you'll probably find you've gained weight.

 **40 mins**

Calories burned:
Unless he's a very energetic masturbator, the cuck derives little slimming benefit from this niche fetish and may well indulge in a comfort eating binge afterwards, while the wife and her 'bull' can expect to shed **100** to **150 kcal** each.

Weight loss bonus:
+50 kcal (half a grapefruit) if the cuck is restrained (and therefore less physically active).

+100 kcal (2 kiwi fruit) for sissy cuck – those calories go straight to his hips.

-50 kcal (15 cherry tomatoes) for the cuck if he's 'hotwifing' (proud to share his hot other half) since a self-esteem boost is always good for the waistline.

Motivational thought:
If you want to be humiliated and lose weight, why not go to the gym instead?

Did you know?
The word 'fetish' comes from
the Portuguese feitico, meaning
'charm' or 'sorcery'.

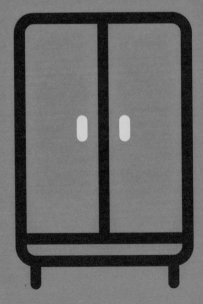

#34 Scissoring

When two women open their legs and grind their junk – that's scissoring, commonly performed lying down, but the range of positions is limited only by your imagination. There's no right or wrong way – just keep smashing those beef curtains together until you both crack your marbles and ideally shift some of that stubborn cellulite.

 35 mins

Calories burned:
When you really go for it, scissoring is as calorie hungry as penetrative straight sex. Expect to burn at least 80 kcal. It's too much effort for some, but great for your core, glutes and thighs.

-5 kcal (4 almonds) if you feel the burn in your abs and lats.

-25 kcal (apple quarter) if your arms start to ache.

-50 kcal (half a fried egg) for all the yoga-origami shit that scissoring entails.

Motivational thought:
Scissoring exists, and it's great!

Did you know?
Controversially, scissoring is the most popular category of all time on PornHub. Critics claim that this demonstrates how scissoring has been co-opted or even invented as a heterosexual male fantasy, like the persistent myth that women sometimes eat bananas or popsicles. However, 40 per cent of the lesbian community would disagree. It remains a popular way for two women to pursue their weight loss goals together.

SCISSORING

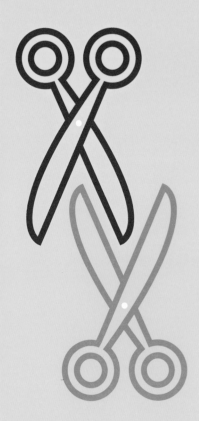

#35 Role Play

In role play, you're limited only by your imagination and your fear of spilling the beans to your partner. It's your chance to explore your wildest sexual fantasies, experiment with the erotic thrill of power dynamics, give expression to your kinks and spice up your sex life.

 **20 mins**

Calories burned:
Think of any scenario or character that turns you on: French maid, nurse, secretary, pretending to be strangers, doctor, gynaecologist, hot teacher, tennis instructor, lumberjack, traffic cop. The novelty and sexier physical and mental experience causes an explosion of happy brain hormones – the same ones that are triggered when you binge eat an entire chocolate cake.

Weight loss bonus:
-100 kcal (half a cantaloupe melon) if you get heavily into cosplay (costumes), whether it's Khaleesi or Sonic the Hedgehog, because that takes more preparation and keeps your mind off snacking.

Motivational thought:
If your sexual fantasies were truly of interest to others, they would no longer be fantasies.
Fran Lebowitz

ROLE PLAY

Did you know?
According to a study published
in the Journal of Sexual Medicine,
76 per cent of men think it's
physically harmful not to have sex.

#36 Doggie Style

Although this feels less intimate than smoochy face humping, being on all fours tones the woman's glutes and quadriceps. He gets to stare at her leather cheerio and then bust his nuts all over her lower back (zero extra calories burned – just saying).

 20 mins

Calories burned:

She burns a gratifying **98 kcals** (4 squares of yummy chocolate); he burns **150 kcals** (14 Original Pringles).

Weight loss bonus:

-5 kcal (1 olive, in brine not oil) for both if he brings in some nipple play.

-25 kcal (half a miso soup sachet) if she grips the headboard, working out the shoulders, biceps and triceps.

-25 kcal (half a dill pickle) if she eats the pillow.

+400 kcal if her bruised knees and cervix make her cry off the gym in the morning.

Motivational thought:

A true friend leaves you with roseate buttcheeks and paw prints on your heart.

Did you know?
Doggie style hits the G-spot
like a boss.

DOGGIE STYLE

#37 Rusty Trombone

For those of you unfamiliar with this manoeuvre, it involves
a little light rimming with a simultaneous two-handed
accompaniment on the meat section. This is definitely not an
entry-level position and it's unsuitable for those of a delicate
disposition.

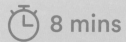 8 mins

Calories burned:
As with any buff and wax, the performer burns about 50 kcals
(35g light soft cheese and celery) extra per hour than the
receiver, only with the possible added frisson of tossing their
cookies or getting bacterial food poisoning.

Weight loss bonus:
-400 kcal (8 miso soup sachets) if the performer
brings up his or her lunch.

-5,000 kcal (100 dill pickles) if the performer
contracts campylobacter.

Motivational thought:
The only thing that ultimately matters is to eat an ice-cream
cone, play a slide trombone, plant a small tree, good God, now
you're free.
Ray Manzarek

Did you know?
For the receiver, the rusty trombone can often
feel like taking part in a threesome.

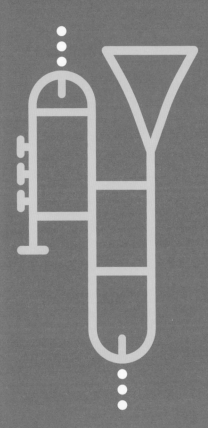

RUSTY TROMBONE

#38 Cowgirl

The woman sits on top of her partner at a 90-degree angle and then bumps and grinds in search of a rhythm while trying to ignore the lactic acid burning at the front of her thighs. This is a workout for her, so the man may offer some optional thrusting from below and try to bust a nut quickly like a true gentleman.

 12 to 25 mins

Calories burned:
The woman burns most of the calories in this multitasking position, and also gets a good core workout if she doesn't use her hands for balance. This leaves them free to pleasure her nips or to dial for fast food. This position is great for clit stimulation, so good for a quickie, but also ideal if she wants to control speed, tempo and depth.

Weight loss bonus:
-200 kcal (2 small handfuls of chocolate kisses) for the thigh, core and buttocks workout.

-20 kcal every time she spells out 'coconut' with her hips.

-25 kcal (half a light cheese triangle) for nip action.

+1,200 kcal for pizza.

Motivational thought:
It's all very simple, keep your mind in the middle and a leg on each side.

Did you know?
Being on top is one of the best
positions for a woman to climax,
plus it allows lots of face-to-face
smoochery if everyone is feeling
loved up.

COWGIRL

— Yeehaw!

#39 Spanking

Whether you're a kink-loving sub or like to dominate, some days you just need a big hug . . . on the perineum with a length of two-by-four. Spanking is customarily the act of striking the buttocks in order to cause physical pain and possible humiliation, using the open hand or tools such as paddles, crops, canes and pasta spoons.

 40 mins

Calories burned:
There are weight loss benefits for both parties but recent studies show that chronic pain reduces appetite and that a high-protein low-carb diet reduces chronic pain. Spanking exploits this intimate relationship between pain and hunger. What greater motivation can there be to ditch the carbs than taking a monumental blistering that reduces your backside to taramosalata?

Weight loss bonus:

-100 kcal (165g pineapple) for both if the spanker gets out of breath.

-700 kcal (25 party ring biscuits) a week if you get a regular daily paddling.

-300 kcal (10 mini milk lollies) for making your giant pasta spoon redundant and simultaneously repurposing it.

-75 kcal (hard-boiled egg) per day that you can't sit down.

Motivational thought:
I'm all for bringing back the birch, but only between consenting adults.

Gore Vidal

Did you know?
Diligent spanking can help
to dissolve the orange peel
fat dimples on the backs of
your thighs.

SPANKING

#40 Pop Your Cherry

Your first consensual penetrative intercourse is more likely to be a fumbling quickie than a tantric all-nighter, so it scores lower than most other activities. If you're left thinking 'Was that it?', then welcome to the club.

 **4 mins**

Calories burned:
You're now officially sexually active. Another rite of passage ticked off. So blow out the candles, turn off the music and . . . whoa, this ride is going too fast. Soon you'll be plucking your first grey hair and buying pruning shears. At least you burned 40 kcals (a very small banana), yey.

Weight loss bonus:
-25 kcal (1 medium carrot) if you cried afterwards.

-100 kcal (cheese-stuffed pitta pocket) if it's in your parents' bed, for laundering sheets and inspecting the headboard for stray pubes.

+1,000 kcal (280 grapes) for all the alcopops you had to drink first.

+5,000 kcal (1.5kg Cheerios) if it's with your needy hometown boy/girlfriend instead of waiting until you escaped this nowhere hellhole.

Motivational thought:
It is an infantile superstition of the human spirit that virginity would be thought a virtue and not the barrier that separates ignorance from knowledge.

Voltaire

Did you know?
In ancient Rome, the Vestal Virgins were high-born priestesses who maintained the eternal flame of Vesta, goddess of the hearth. Selected in childhood, they took a 30-year vow of chastity, after which they retired and were allowed to marry.

POP YOUR CHERRY

#41 Titty Wank

This traditionally favours women with the larger frontage, but in this era of post-truth sexual politics, there's no reason why even a pair of beagle ears should preclude a grateful human male from grinding a furrow with his purple hampton until he sprays warm blooge into her hair and environs while she screams her approval.

 12 mins

Calories burned:
Women with smaller breasts experience a stronger tricep and forearm workout, as they have to apply greater lateral force to prevent off-roading. Calories burned can be calculated by assigning the cup size with a number (AA=19, A=18, B=17 ... LL=2, M=1) and then multiplying its square root by the number of minutes.

Weight loss bonus:

-40 kcals (half an apple) towelling down/showering afterwards.

-800 kcals (16 large plums) steam cleaning the curtains and having the dog professionally shampooed.

-2,000 kcals (79 marshmallows) choosing and hanging replacement wallpaper.

Motivational thought:
'Wow, Claire has prima facie boobs, I would love to...'

TITTY WANK

Did you know?
Despite what you might have seen on the Internet and the erotic wall art of Pompeii and Herculaneum, fake boobs (aka breast implants) are reputed to be too inflexible for a trip down mammary lane.

#42 Swaffelen

Saucy French philosopher Michel Foucault famously rejected the 'repressive hypothesis' of sexuality but even he failed to place swaffelen into its proper social context. Indeed, one can say with a high degree of confidence that in his seminal four-volume study of western sexuality, the phrase 'turkey slap' makes not a single appearance. Today it remains a niche, even taboo subject, probably due to a perceived power imbalance.

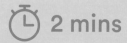 2 mins

Calories burned:
-10 kcal (2½ jelly beans) each per five mins of swaffelen.

Weight loss bonus:
-4,900 kcal (98 rich tea biscuits) expended persuading your partner to let you do it (see below).

Motivational thought:
Everyone should be respected as an individual, but no one idolized.
Albert Einstein

Did you know?
Being gently swatted in the face by a semi-erect boner can be interpreted as a profoundly intellectual and transformative act, a confident neo-feminist assertion of the potency of cultural relativism.

SWAFFELEN

#43 Thigh Job

The thigh job smacks of foreplay or dry humping – the man places his yomper between a woman's thighs and starts pumping. You can thigh hump in several positions including cowgirl, spooning, missionary, doggy or standing but make sure you use plenty of lube.

 8 mins

Calories burned:
Check out the positions elsewhere in this book for the calorie-burning figures and then subtract 20 kcal for being so tantalisingly close to her love box without actually scoring.

Weight loss bonus:
-5 kcal (1 roasted peanut) every time she accidentally clamps his crotch nuggets.

-50 kcal (1 Oreo) for shaping and toning her leg and hip muscles.

+100 kcal (half an avocado) for whoever has to sleep in the wet patch.

Motivational thought:
Lie down, lie easy. Let me shipwreck in your thighs.
Dylan Thomas

Did you know?
A thigh job is also called 'femoral
intercourse', named after the femur
(thigh) bone. The inner upper thigh
is a major erogenous zone and is
packed with nerve endings.

THIGH JOB

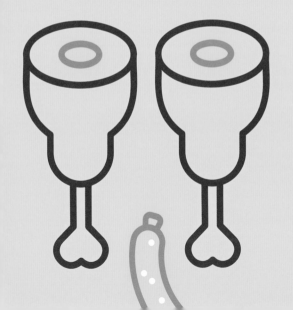

#44 The Wheelbarrow

The woman kneels with her elbows flat on the floor in front of her. The standing man picks her up by the thighs and wears her like a codpiece, while she clamps her ankles behind his back. He supplies all the thrusting while she wonders if all this effort is worthwhile just to keep the relationship alive.

 **12 mins**

Calories burned:
Both parties get a targeted workout and burn about 100 kcals. She tenses her inner thigh muscles and uses her arms to stop her from breaking her teeth on the floor. Unless she works her abdominals hard, she'll start to sink and lose the deep penetration, so for her there's good motivation baked into this position. He gets burning thighs and an upper body workout as he grips her waist to stop her from sliding away.

Weight loss bonus:
-40 kcal (1 wholegrain crispbread) if she has to keep batting away an inquisitive family pet.

-500 kcal (15 cheese and pickle canapés) if she orders a half-size portion the next time she visits a restaurant so she can escape The Wheelbarrow for two months.

Motivational thought:
If sex is dignified it's not being done right.
J D Robb

THE WHEELBARROW

Did you know?
After staring at the same worn patch for ten minutes, if she wants an excuse to change the carpet, this position offers good stimulation for her A-spot (the anterior fornix erogenous zone) which can bring on a powerful vaginal ejaculation.

#45 Face Sitting

Also known as queening or kinging, this sexual practice has a spectrum of calorie-burning options. Being at altitude causes weight loss without any additional effort; face sitting provides similar hypoxic benefits. The sitter can also increase his or her calorie consumption by performing a few core-strengthening exercises or by cumming like a standpipe.

 15 mins

Calories burned:
An average person working at a desk burns about 100 calories an hour, so that's the minimum a passive sitter can expect to lose. Squatting burns an additional 120 calories an hour, or just relax and shizzle your grundel butter like a porn star.

Weight loss bonus:
-80 kcal (4 large scallops) as you sit, bend your knees towards your chest and out again whilst leaning back. This is great for your abs, but may leave your partner needing reconstructive facial surgery.

-30 kcal (7 baby carrots) for laughing continuously as you grind your posterior into your partner's face.

Motivational thought:
Gravitation is the lust of the cosmos.
Mary Roach

FACE SITTING

Did you know?
Online pornography that depicts face sitting was banned in the United Kingdom in 2014.

Footnote

The author points out that you should know by now (because by now you have studied the book from cover to cover) that many of the facts have obviously been **entirely made up** – but not quite all of them, so part of the fun is working out which ludicrous assertion is, in fact, a fact.

The cliché goes that fact is stranger than fiction, but it might mess with your head to know that although for legal purposes this is a work of complete fiction, all but one of the 'Did you know' facts are true, or can at least be subjectively argued. Also, even though lots of the calorie burning has been guestimated or exaggerated for comic effect, it has been based on actual science and wherever kcals appear as their comestible equivalent, they are fairly accurate – for example, 80 kcal does equal 4 large scallops.

You are welcome to test all this science with your own detailed critical examinations, observations, evaluations or trials: meticulous peer review of this statistical hypothesis will ultimately lead to its proof or disproof and to its acceptance or rejection. Regardless, you might have some fun trying this out.

Acknowledgements

The author would also like to have thanked friends & family, but if they were named, then the author would surely be disowned, ostracised, and disinherited.

In truth, the author would also have loved to make an acknowledgement to world experts in this field, though can't, because there don't appear to be any worth mentioning.

Index

The author would like to suggest a reading list of seminal books on this subject, but for some reason there aren't any.

So the author would like to assert that this tome is now the 'bible' on this subject, and should become required reading for anyone interested in either sex and/or dieting.